WRITE IN ANOTHER LANGUAGE

TEN EASY STEPS

HELENA HALME

To Yen
For all your
help & support!
[illegible]

COPYRIGHT

e-ISBN: 978-0-9957495-3-5
ISBN: 978-0-9957495-4-2

Visit www.helenahalme.com for more books by the same author and for news and reviews of Helena's work.

CONTENTS

INTRODUCTION

Why Do I Write in English?

When I tell people I'm a writer, the first thing they ask me apart from what I write (Nordic contemporary fiction) is what language I use. Apart from my thesis, which I wrote in Swedish, I've written all of my eleven books in English. When I tell them this, the next query inevitably is: "Why not Finnish or Swedish?"

English is one of the most widely spoken, and certainly read, languages in the world, so it makes sense to write in English. But there are other reasons why I choose to use what technically amounts to my third language.

My mother tongue is Finnish, a language spoken by just 5 million people. It's said to be one of the most difficult languages to learn, along with Mandarin, Arabic, and Japanese.

Because of its difficulty, and the small number of people who speak it, most Finns learn another language early on in their lives. They go on to learn at least one more language, and sometimes are fluent in many.

A perfect example of Finnish multilingualism was recently given by Finland's former Prime Minister Alexander Stubb, now MEP (Member of the European Parliament). When stepping out of his car in Brussels, he was interviewed by three different news reporters, in three of the five languages he speaks. Without hesitation, he turned from one to the other, switching from German to French to English without a single umm or ahh.

My language skills aren't quite this impressive. I speak only three languages. I started studying English at my school in Tampere, a town in central Finland, at the age of seven. When I was eleven, my family moved to Stockholm and I became fluent in Swedish.

I don't remember the moment when I began to understand the Swedish-speaking pupils around me, but I vividly recall the first day at my new school in Stockholm. It was late August and hot underneath the plastic canopy that connected four brightly colored buildings, when my mother handed me over to the care of a diminutive, nervous woman.

It turned out that my new teacher had reason to be jumpy; during my very first lesson at my new school I witnessed something that shocked me to the core. The teacher, whom I later found to be a kindhearted, timid woman, was bullied by 20 or so rowdy pre-teens. During that lesson, she had to duck to avoid a ruler thrown by a particularly nasty long-haired boy sitting at the back of the class. I also saw another boy kick my new teacher, while she—without success—tried to bring the class to heel.

In Finland, school was rather different. Good

behavior was drummed into pupils from an early age, and I couldn't escape its shackles. That classroom was never quiet and I was glad to escape to my daily language lessons with a Finnish teacher who was the opposite of my class teacher. Large, loud, and full of stories about her ailments, from sinusitis to indigestion, she provided me with the key to my scary new world—Swedish.

My next memory after that first, unsettling day was of making friends with a fellow (well-behaved) pupil called Anna. Suddenly I was able to converse with my new friend without difficulty, and I could understand the praise showered on me by my new teacher. I think I must have been naturally talented at languages, too, because after just a few months nobody could tell that I hadn't been born in Stockholm.

I've been told by my mother and sister that we used to practice the strange, Swedish, pronunciation at home, to ensure that no one would know we were from Finland (the discrimination against Finns in Sweden was legendary in those days, but that's another story). However, I have no memory of these practice sessions. When we moved back to Finland four years later, I had to relearn my mother tongue. All through this period, I was also learning English.

After taking my Baccalaureate in a Finnish school in Helsinki, I studied economics at a Swedish language university in Finland. After graduation, at the tender age of 22, I moved to Britain. Almost as soon as I arrived, I began writing a diary. At first, I wrote in Finnish, but when it became difficult to describe what was happening around me in my mother tongue, I turned the notebook over and began writing in English. Eventually, the English language side took over.

Although a language history like mine isn't particularly unusual in Finland, or in the rest of the multilingual and multicultural world of today, the ability to speak several languages has certainly given me opportunities that I otherwise wouldn't have had. For one, I feel at home in several countries and cultures. Whenever I visit Stockholm, it feels as if I've come home, even though I moved back to Finland at the age of fourteen. I feel a similar sense of belonging in Tampere, Helsinki, Portsmouth, and London.

Multiculturalism is Good

If you're an author, being able to blend into your surroundings is an invaluable tool. Writers are the world's great observers and what's better than being able to listen to conversations in the local tongue of a "foreign" country and then make up stories based on what you've heard and seen for a new audience? I often feel that had I not moved countries so many times, I would not have the compulsion to write.

Conversely, this ability to move easily from one culture to another also produces a certain degree of detachment. Feeling as though you belong to several cultures often makes you an observer in all of them. There is also the issue of language discrimination, but I will talk more about the language we speak and how it affects our behavior later.

This book is mainly aimed at fiction writers, but if you are planning to write a nonfiction book, or a regular blog, you will find it useful too. All writing is, after all, essentially storytelling.

In this book, I share a number of practical tips that you can use to make writing in another language easier, whether it's fiction or nonfiction.

1

WHAT IS LANGUAGE?

A language is a system of communication which consists of a set of sounds and written symbols which are used by the people of a particular country or region for talking or writing. (Collins English Dictionary)

In other words, language is a hugely powerful and essential tool that we humans use to communicate with each other.

Language also appertains to a particular nation or people. There are about 7,000 different tongues spoken in the world today (*Ethnologue*, published by SIL International). This amount is diminishing by the day—some say that in 100 years' time we will have lost half that number.

Bilingualism

Around half of the world's population describe themselves as bilingual, and many people speak several languages fluently. There are those who have been brought up using two languages and there are those, like me, who learned a second language early in their lives. I was eleven when my family moved to Sweden and my parents, thinking they were doing the right thing, enrolled me and my thirteen-year-old sister into a wholly Swedish-speaking school.

Whether the culture shock was so dramatic that I have completely blocked out my memory of struggling to speak Swedish, or whether I was incredibly fast at learning the language, I do not know. Mastering another language at a young age, however, accelerated my natural aptitude for learning other languages.

Language and Behavior

There's a lot of debate about the usefulness of speaking several languages, and how this affects our beliefs and ways of thinking. Charlemagne, the Holy Roman Emperor, said, "To Have another language is to possess a second soul," while in *Romeo and Juliet*, Shakespeare writes, "A rose by any other name would smell as sweet," suggesting the language spoken doesn't make any difference to one's emotions.

In a recent study, it was found that using a language that is not your mother tongue affects your decision-making, reducing emotional reactivity and leading to an increase in utilitarian judgments. Researchers asked their subjects whether they'd sacrifice one man to save five.

> *Should you sacrifice one man to save five? Whatever your answer, it should not depend on whether you were asked the question in your native language or a foreign tongue so long as you understood the problem. And yet*

> *here we report evidence that people using a foreign language make substantially more utilitarian decisions when faced with such moral dilemmas. We argue that this stems from the reduced emotional response elicited by the foreign language, consequently reducing the impact of intuitive emotional concerns. In general, we suggest that the increased psychological distance of using a foreign language induces utilitarianism. This shows that moral judgments can be heavily affected by an orthogonal property to moral principles, and importantly, one that is relevant to hundreds of millions of individuals on a daily basis. (*Albert Costa and Boaz Keysar, *Your Morals Depend on Language*, PlosOne, April 2014.)

This is an interesting study to consider for anyone thinking about writing in another language. If your deep moral judgments are affected by the language you use, it therefore must follow that writing in that language makes you more detached from the work.

In a TED talk in November 2017, the cognitive scientist Lera Boroditsky claims that language has a big, deep, early, broad, and weighty effect on the human brain. Boroditsky sites examples of languages where time is expressed in a completely different way, a tongue where numbers aren't used, or where the color blue has a different name if it's a light or a dark shade.

Another example of how language affects how we behave and see things is the use of the neutral form when describing an event. In English, for example, we can say "I broke my arm," whereas in Spanish we'd say "My arm broke." If you say that you yourself broke your arm in Spanish, it would seem as if you went out of your way to harm yourself, which would be classified as a very disturbed action.

The way the Spanish describe events make those speaking the language look differently at what has happened. In English, we attribute some responsibility to an individual for an event, while in Spanish it "just happens." Again, this shows how the language we speak has a great influence on how we look at the world, and how we write about it. (TED talk by Lera Boroditsky, November, 2017)

My Mother Tongue

I can certainly relate to Ms. Boroditsky's research. Finnish, my mother tongue, spoken by only about 5 million people, is a completely different language from those of its Scandinavian neighbors. In Finnish, we often express ideas in a very different way from the more commonly studied European languages. We have thirteen cases, there are no prepositions, and most words change shape when spoken in a different context.

I often say that that I would not be able to write anything in Finnish without becoming upset. For me, my mother tongue is almost too emotional. My feeling validates the research of Costa et al (see p 4). I'm not sure if I would send that one man to his death, but certainly I know that my reactions when speaking Finnish are based more on my emotions than they are when I'm communicating in English.

Another difference between Finnish and English is that Finnish has no grammatical gender. It is completely gender-neutral as it has no distinct female and male pronouns like "he" or "she," but a common gender-neutral "hän." This lack of gender is quite significant when writing fiction in Finnish. You have to work a lot harder at letting the reader know which character is speaking, or whose thoughts and emotions you are describing.

Interestingly, Sweden has introduced a similar gender-neutral pronoun into its modern language. Swedes are now encouraged to use "hen" instead of "han" (male) or "hon" (female). This shows how Sweden has recognized the importance language has on attitudes and behavior. They are allowing language to develop and purposefully adopt ideas from other cultures to meet the needs of a modern society.

Understanding Different Languages is Powerful

To understand how language shapes the way we think is incredibly enriching. To speak another language—or more than one—truly enables you to comprehend the world and how different people think.

For writers, this additional knowledge is powerful. It enables us to see the world from various angles and describe the human experience in new and exciting ways.

To understand and write in another language is thrilling and fulfilling, and will produce an enriching experience for the reader.

There are many examples in historical as well as modern literature of authors writing in a language that is not their own. Some do it to gain a wider readership, others for political or personal reasons. They may not wish their nearest and dearest to read their words, for example. Or they may need to be inspired by a fresh perspective. Some do it just to be able to use a different style. Using different languages enriches your life and will also enhance your writing.

A Brief Overview of Modern English

Modern English spread around the world through the influence of the British Empire between the 17th and mid-20th centuries. Spurred on by the emergence of the United States as a global superpower, English became the leading language of international discourse and the *lingua franca* in many professional contexts, such as science, navigation, and law. (*Wikipedia*)

English is the third most-spoken native language in the world, after Standard Chinese and Spanish. It is the most widely learned second language and is either the official language or one of the official languages in almost 60 sovereign states. There are more people who have learned English as a second language than there are native speakers. English is the most commonly spoken language in the United Kingdom, the United States, Canada, Australia, Ireland, and New Zealand, and it is widely spoken in some areas of the Caribbean, Africa, and South Asia. It is a co-official language of the United Nations, the European Union and many other world and regional international organizations. It is the most widely spoken Germanic language, accounting for at least 70 percent of speakers of this Indo-European branch. English has a vast vocabulary, though counting how many words any language has is impossible. (*Wikipedia*)

It's therefore understandable that many authors choose to write in English even when it's their second or third language. But even if your aim isn't to reach a larger readership, writing in another language can be a useful tool to give you a unique voice, or inspire your creativity.

2

LANGUAGE PREJUDICE

Using a language that is not your mother tongue is not all good news.

Particularly with the spoken word, there is a common phenomenon called *linguicism*, a term coined in the 1980s by a Finnish linguist Tove Skutnabb-Kangas. This phenomenon refers to linguistic discrimination against somebody based on their use of language. It can include their vocabulary, their accent, or their use of grammar. Links between a lack of education and language have been used as justification for oppression and control of people by the dominant ruling classes throughout history.

In general in the UK, standard southern accents are considered to be more acceptable than other accents. Welsh, Scottish, and Newcastle accents are regarded as friendly and trustworthy, while others are sometimes looked down upon as a sign of a lack of intelligence. Research has shown that more than a quarter of Britons feel discriminated against because of their accent. (ComRes poll for ITV, September 25, 2013)

Teachers feel they need to change their accent to be taken more seriously, and teachers with northern accents have even been told to "posh up." (Dr. Alexander Baratta, *the Guardian*, May 12, 2016)

Experts in their field face prejudice because of their accents—including academics who feel they can't be taken seriously with, say, a northern English accent. (Gerry Howley, University of Sheffield for *The Conversation*, May 3, 2017)

Even masters of their craft have been typecast and

discriminated against because of their speech. Acclaimed British actor Maxine Peake, for example, was told to lose her Bolton accent when auditioning for a character who had been to university. (*The iNews*, April 29, 2017)

Even in Finland, someone from a northern county is seen as stupid, while a person from eastern Finland is thought wily, and anyone with a Helsinki accent is considered snobbish.

In the UK, those speaking with regional accents often describe themselves as sounding "common." On the other hand, privately educated "posh boys" are now adopting regional accents, such as "Estuary English" to make themselves more "authentic" and popular.

Such prejudices reveal a staggering level of ignorance. The fact that notions of a "common," "bad," or "correct" accent are imposed by society eludes most people. Received pronunciation based on educated speech in southern England is still considered superior.

In the US, a study showed that some potential employers, real estate agents, loan officers, and service providers linguistically profile callers responding to adverts, despite this being against federal and state law. (John Baugh, Ph.D., the Margaret Bush Wilson Professor and Director of African and African American Studies in Arts & Sciences, Washington University in St. Louis, February 2, 2006)

Why can't we shake our prejudices about dialects? Part of the problem is that these attitudes are so deeply ingrained within us that we all tend to believe them. Our standard language ideology maintains that standard accents are associated with class, privilege, education, and opportunity.

Despite former British prime minister John Major's 1990 declaration that he wanted Britain to be a classless society, recent evidence indicates that class divisions are just as wide as before. The 2016 Brexit Referendum brought discrimination based on both race and accent to the surface. During the campaign the leading Brexiteer, Nigel Farage, said he felt "awkward" on a train journey in central London when he heard only foreign languages being spoken by his fellow passengers. (*London Evening Standard*, February 28, 2014)

Unfortunately, it seems that linguistic discrimination really is one of society's last acceptable forms of prejudice.

My Experience

Speaking with a Nordic accent was often looked upon favorably when I first moved to Britain in the early 1980s. We Scandinavians (or Nordics, as Finland is strictly not part of the Scandinavian peninsula) were viewed as well-educated, honest —and sexy. I was also in possession of blue eyes and blonde hair, so it seemed I was fair game to any British male who fancied chatting me up— and worse. I soon learned to cast my eyes downwards, and when opening my mouth to speak I would introduce the fact that I was (newly) married as soon as possible.

As far as the writing goes, I was introduced to *linguicism* the first time I read a piece of my fiction at a critique session on an MA Course in Creative Writing. The format for the class was simple: each of the six students would read out a piece of up to 1,000 words and then the others would critique the work while the author was obliged to remain quiet.

When it was my turn, I read a piece from my first (unpublished) novel. The story was a psychological thriller in which a family's nanny tries to usurp the mother by making herself irreplaceable to the husband and children. In the middle of the book, the nanny is found hanging from the rafters of a barn, and the question is: did she kill herself or did someone have it in for her? (The untitled manuscript was dubbed *The Hanging Nanny* by my MA class, so even if I decided to edit and publish this particular story, I'd struggle to give it another, better, title.)

I'd spent some time writing the novel, and many hours editing the piece and reading it aloud, so I was pretty confident it would be well received. "Sounds like a translation," was the first comment I received from a fellow would-be writer. After the class, I asked what the person had meant by the statement. He shook his head: "I'm not sure, but it just didn't sound quite right to me. You know. Like foreign books—which I never read, because I hate translations."

At the time, this comment completely floored me. I knew that I couldn't change the way I wrote—my style. It didn't even occur to me that my fellow student's opinion was based partly (or wholly?) on my accent. Before being accepted on the MA course, I'd also read many articles, written by language experts, stating that that an author, however talented, cannot write well in a language that is not their mother tongue. Luckily, I went on to have many successful readings. I was frequently complimented on my work and on one occasion even compared to Vladimir Nabokov, who wrote *Lolita* in his third language! (I've dined out on the comment for a while now.)

Today, I'm lucky to have a solid readership, with thousands of readers enjoying my books worldwide. My books are bought by people in 73 countries, according to the latest report, for which I am incredibly proud and grateful.

As you embark on your writing adventure, you must remember that sometimes those who've never mastered another language cannot understand that writing in another language is not as hard and certainly not as absurd as they think. On the contrary, it's enriching and thrilling.

3

YOU ARE UNIQUE

Using another language in communication, be it written or spoken, affects the way we behave and feel about our actions.

You may have noticed that we find it a lot easier to swear or use rude words in another language. Anything taboo is easy to pick up in a second language and entertaining to use.

Perhaps you remember how, when learning another language at school, the first words we all wanted the teacher to tell us were the rude ones?

Boys in the back of my English class would shout out swear words as a joke. Had they been using these words in Finnish, I think there would have been a few detentions handed out, but because they were uttered in another language, everyone, even the teacher (up to a point), found it just a little funny.

This detachment from taboo words is indicative of the greater emotional distance that using a foreign language provides. While this detachment can make it easier for us to say rather distasteful things, recent studies have shown that it can also affect our perception of morality.

During research carried out by Costa et al (see Chapter 1) it was found that violations of social norms, such as saying a white lie to get a reduced fare, became easier in another language. This change of behavior might be explained by facilitated deliberation, misunderstanding, or the adoption of a universalistic stance. The researchers were convinced, however, that people's social and moral norms were less sensitive when making judgments in another language (such as sacrificing one man to save five others). The decision-making process is a slower and more deliberate cost-benefit judgment. In other words, decisions made in a foreign language are not as susceptible to emotional biases as those made in a native language. This means that you gain an increased degree of detachment when writing in another language. Your brain lacks the normal judgments shaped by the long-held traditions and experiences of native speakers.

Detachment

Detachment from the usual moral and social judgments can be a huge advantage when telling a story. It means that your voice is different and your work unique. Let me explain what I mean.

When writing in another language, you often use a different way to describe people, places, and events. Your judgment of them depends on the social norms you've inherited from your native country, or your upbringing. Of course, this is the same for someone from a different social class writing in their mother tongue, but the creative possibilities are even greater for someone writing in another language.

Not only are the words different, but a writer using a foreign language also sees events and places differently. For example, the Tube, which a London commuter will consider as a dirty and noisy place they need to use in order to get to work each morning, will seem cool, or even romantic, to a tourist.

Similarly, when living away from your home, places and traditions often gain a rosy glow to you. If there are painful memories from home, they are easier to describe using another language. You thus gain a degree of detachment.

Naturally, it's important that we can communicate

with our readers, and this is why it's vital that we check our work before we send it out into the world, but can you see how writing in another language creates huge opportunities for the creative mind?

I often say that one of the reasons I don't write in Finnish is because if I did, I'd probably be crying all the time. My books are quite emotional and I often go into deep, dark places to discover the true emotions of my characters. In English, I am able to remain more detached, almost as if watching my characters move independently of me. There's a movie reel in front of me and all I have to do is to write down what happens. I have a certain distance from my story, which I know is only there because I write in English.

Many authors describe the writing process in a similar way, even if they use their native tongue. However, when writing in a foreign language, the detachment is heightened.

. . .

Positive Detachment

You can also use vocabulary and scenes that are more extreme than those that native speakers might use. You can become bolder and braver in your descriptions and expressions. If you are writing a story based on real events, your sense of being exposed in revealing your true emotions or those of the characters in your story (be they fictional or "real") is more controlled. You can delve deeper into the characters' motivations and feelings without the unconscious sense of judgment inherited from your own culture via the native language.

As a non-native writer, you see the world around you with fresh eyes. This vision can result in unusual interpretations of the human condition. Isn't this what all writers dream about? Being able to describe characters, places, and events in your books in a new way?

Negative Detachment

On the other hand, you may overshoot with your

characters' actions and emotions. It is possible to alienate your audience by being too honest, too violent, too sensual, and so on. But this heightened way of writing may become your particular style, which will set you apart from the other writers in your genre. Difference, as long as you are able to communicate with your readership, is always good.

Being too forceful in your writing may offend the sensibilities of the readers in the country where the language is spoken. However, with an international readership this is rarely an issue. If, for example, you write in English, and this is your non-native language, you are sure to find an audience in the many other non-native speakers, or regions where English is spoken, even if you come across as *too* radical in Britain.

The biggest advantage of writing in a foreign language is the different voice you can achieve as a writer. But there are many other ways you can make use of this "foreigness".

. . .

Set Your Story in Your Native Country

As writers, we are told to "write what you know." At the same time readers often ask for books that "take them somewhere new." So why not use your uniqueness to your advantage and set a book in the country or countries in which you grew up? Your experiences from your home will be tremendously interesting to people in other countries. Share your authentic viewpoint and tell a story set in the place you know intimately.

You can make all or some of your characters the same nationality as you, or let someone from your new adopted country (or language) come and live or visit your home. As a person who has experienced life in more than one country, you are in a wonderful position to show how your home country looks to outsiders, as well as what it's like to live there.

You are in a unique position to tell the story of someone who decides to (or is forced) to live somewhere else. What culture clashes did you encounter when you moved to your new country? What did you miss from home? Food, ways of doing things like queueing for buses or visiting doctors may seem mundane to you, but these details are excellent in capturing the differences between countries and cultures.

In my latest novel, *The Island Affair*, the main character, Alicia, returns to the Nordic islands where she grew up, together with her English husband, Liam. In this way I use both my familiarity with the setting, the Åland Islands, and my understanding of how it feels to live abroad for a long time while always longing to go back. I also describe Liam's response to his wife's home. The quaintness of the Islands isn't quite as charming to him as it is to Alicia.

Equally, if you've lived away from your home country for a while you will have an outsider's view of home. You can describe people, places, history, and culture with a stranger's eyes, while at the same time being an expert in them. Can you see how all of these factors will make what you write hugely engaging and different from any other author's work?

Describe Your Displacement

Lastly, in this section I want to discuss your ability as a "foreign" author to describe the differences between your adopted country and other places. Again, this will be particular to you. Use this ability to see the countries you've lived in through a stranger's eyes. You notice things that those who have been born there do not.

Make one of your characters the same nationality as you and describe living in the new place through his or her eyes. Again, this ability to look at your new country with detachment adds richness. Many other authors, particularly those who've never lived abroad, will envy your in-depth knowledge of displacement. As I have said before, to have a new and distinctive viewpoint of the human condition is what all authors seek.

What's more, many people move from one country to another, but very few decide to take the often scary step of writing about their experiences. So, be bold, be brave, and use the unique viewpoint and voice you have as an author writing in another language.

Authenticity

Your ability to describe both your home country and your displacement in your new adopted home will give your work authenticity. To add to this, don't shy away from using local words and expressions when describing your home country. They add spice to the story and deepen the reader's sense of being transported to a new—very different—place.

Famous Authors Writing in Another Language

There is a long tradition of authors gaining new readerships by switching languages. If you decide to write in English, which is still one of the world's most popular languages, you can massively increase the size of your readership. Many authors have done this.

Vladimir Nabokov wrote *Lolita* in English, his third language. His trilingual upbringing had a profound influence on his work. The richness of his language and his unique perspective on America—his adopted country—helped make him the darling of the literary world.

Joseph Conrad, a Polish-British writer, didn't speak English until his early twenties. Yet he's considered one of the greatest novelists in the English language. Conrad used his multinationalism to explore the human condition and to write stories with a non-English sensibility.

Karen Blixen was a Danish author writing in Danish, French, and English. Blixen is best known for *Out of Africa*, an account of her life in Kenya. Blixen wrote the book in English and then rewrote it in Danish.

. . .

Turkish novelist **Elif Shafak** is an award-winning author of *The Bastard of Istanbul* and *The Forty Rules of Love*. She writes in English and in Turkish and has taught at different universities around the world, most recently at St. Anne's College of Oxford University.

4

READING

When I began writing in English, I didn't give up reading books in Finnish and Swedish. I'd sometimes add a novel by a French author too, just to try to keep that language alive in my mind. I loved reading a book in its original language; sometimes so much is lost in translation (no pun intended).

But during the year of my MA in Creative Writing at Bath Spa University, when we read a new book every week, I found that my English became better and more fluent. The improvement in my writing was obviously also a result of the regular writing demanded by the course. I hadn't written on a daily basis before, apart from a few notes in my diary.

Then something strange happened. After the course, I found that if I read a book in Finnish or Swedish it was harder to switch to writing in English. Even going on an extended visit to Finland or Sweden, or having friends or family visit me in London, had the same effect on my writing. It would always take a few days before I could get back to my writing and the same level of fluency in the English language. As a trial, I decided to give up any "foreign" language books, and discovered that my English improved again.

If I am in the middle of writing a novel, or a nonfiction title (which nowadays is all the time), I find it particularly disruptive to read longer works in Finnish or Swedish. One day, I may be able to go back to reading books in Finnish and Swedish. As I am now on book eleven (nine fiction titles and two nonfiction titles), I'm not sure this will ever happen.

There has, however, been an improvement in recent years. I've noticed that speaking Finnish regularly doesn't affect my writing much at all, so let's hope the same will happen with reading Finnish and Swedish books. To be truthful, I miss reading fiction in its original tongue. Of course, this may just be me. You may be not be affected by juggling several languages at the same time. There are multilingual authors who can switch languages easily.

Emmi Itäranta, a Finnish-born author based in the UK, constantly reads books in several languages while also writing her own books, chapter by chapter, in two languages. When I found this out, I was amazed. And a little jealous.

Talking about her work, Emmi described a process that hadn't even occurred to me. She writes a chapter in Finnish, puts it aside and proceeds to write the same chapter in English. She does almost a simultaneous translation while writing. Ever since I met this particular author, I have been intrigued by her process.

“I feel that both languages are my tools, with which I can view the text from two slightly different viewpoints.” (An interview with Emmi Itäranta for *YLE News*, February 19, 2017. Translated from Finnish.)

This comment echoes both the sense of detachment and uniqueness that writing in another language provides and which I’ve been exploring in this book. Emmi goes further than just writing in another language, though. She improves the text and the story through her ability to speak and understand two languages.

Other authors I know who write in English as a second or third language are just as strict about their exposure to other languages as I am. In the penultimate chapter of this book, four authors who write in another language share their experiences and tips on writing in a language that is not their mother tongue. My recommendation if you are starting out, writing your first novel or nonfiction title in another language, is to put aside your native tongue. Completely immersing yourself in the language you are going to use will boost your writing immensely.

Try having a few weeks or months away from your native language and see how this forced removal from your mother tongue affects your writing. Then go back to reading books in your mother tongue and see if it makes any difference to your work. Please do let me know what you find out. I'm always intrigued to learn about the writing processes of authors who write in a language that is not their own.

5

CHECK, CHECK, AND RECHECK

Good grammar might seem old-fashioned, but readers still care about correct use of language, even if they may not know it. Mistakes in the text can stop the reader from *suspending disbelief*. I will talk later about this important concept. Similarly, if you are looking for a literary agent or publisher for your work, it's vital that your work is clear of errors.

Turn in a "Clean" Copy

When writing in a language that is not your mother tongue it's even more important to get the grammar and the language right than if you were writing in your native language. Whether we like it or not, once a literary agent, a reader, a reviewer, or a publisher knows you're not writing in your mother tongue, they will be looking for evidence of your inadequacies. This may be *linguicism,* or language discrimination, but we have to be realistic. Readers need to hear the "foreign voice" but not be jarred by it.

The only way to arm yourself against prejudice is to turn in "clean" copy.

This, incidentally, applies to anything you write: social media posts, blogs, articles in magazines, newsletters, as well as your manuscripts. Of course, errors will appear, especially in Twitter posts written in haste on a bus, but try to check your text more than you would if it was in your mother tongue. It's more time-consuming, I know, but it's necessary if you want to be taken seriously as a writer in another language. Even if you are looking to use a specific style, which is completely new, it's important to follow the basic rules of grammar and spelling.

Suspending Disbelief

Nothing puts a potential reader off your text more than incorrect use of language. A wrong preposition, a spelling mistake, or misuse of a proverb will remind the reader that they are reading someone else's words. And that this someone isn't writing in their mother tongue. An error will break the spell of the story, and ultimately will make the reader stop reading and cast your book aside. The reader has stopped *suspending disbelief*. Let me explain further.

A storyteller, whether that's a movie maker, theater director, visual artist, or a writer, want the consumer of the art to get so immersed in the work that they will forget they are reading or watching something that someone else has made up. For the writer, the ultimate goal is for readers to get so involved in the story that they start to talk about the characters as if they really existed.

Recently, I had a negative review of one of my books in *The Nordic Heart* series. Even though the reader gave the book three stars (which is good enough, but not brilliant), she was livid. She felt my main character was lazy, ignorant, and selfish. She wrote a long piece about how the female protagonist ignored her husband and had loose morals.

In spite of its negative tone, I love this review. It shows that the reader had really engaged with my main characters. Fair enough, she didn't like either of them—Peter was "dim" and Kaisa "self-absorbed"—but she talks about them as if they were *real*. This reader had suspended disbelief, which after all was my ultimate goal.

As a writer, even if you write about characters who some readers might hate, you must do everything you can to make sure the reader is kept enthralled by the story, spellbound by the world you have created. Errors such as spelling mistakes, a wrong tense or verb will break this spell and bring the reader back to reality. There are other parts of the story that could also stop the reader from suspending their disbelief, but I'll deal with these later on.

There are many online tools that you can use to check that your work is correct, idiomatic English, but I find this is the easiest part of the writing process. (More about the tools in the next chapter.) More difficult is the use of common expressions and sayings.

The Poirot Method

Sometimes you can add some incorrect language usage to show your character's personality and origin. Agatha Christie's Poirot is well known for getting little British colloquialisms wrong, but Christie knew what she was doing. These "mistakes" in his English language are by no means accidental, but a way to establish the character of Poirot, together with his particular dress sense, obsessive cleanliness, and dislike of English food.

Many authors use this method to distinguish their characters. They may just use a local or foreign accent without actual error. If you write about your home country or nationals, you can have a field day with this method. You, more than anyone, will know exactly what common mistakes your countrymen and women make. However, you must make sure these mistakes are clearly made by the characters and that the rest of the copy is clean.

So check, check, and recheck your spelling, grammar, and any common expressions you are using.

Specific Terminology

In addition to spelling, grammar, sayings, and expressions, there are many areas of specific terminology that you must be careful to get right.

Several scenes in my latest novel, *The Island Affair,* take place on a sailing boat. Majority of the characters in the book are also born on the group of islands, where the story is set, so I had to write knowledgeably about boating terms. Luckily, my husband is ex-Navy, however, some of the specific sailing terms I had to find online and via other friends. When writing from the point of view of a person whose whole life has been spent at sea in one form or another, I had to sound like an expert. (I talk more about using research and experts in Chapter 8.)

Similarly, the use of modern slang, terminology for romantic encounters, or even the descriptions of a corpse have to ring true to your readers. Of course, you can translate an expression, word for word, from a foreign language if the character is foreign, but you have to let your reader know that you are using an expression that is not commonly used in the English language (if the 'other' language you're writing is English). It's important that you don't alienate your reader by taking them away from the story with a saying or a word that doesn't sound right. Don't forget you need your reader to suspend disbelief.

. . .

Conrad and Nabokov

Joseph Conrad and Vladimir Nabokov, two well-known "foreign" authors who wrote in English, use complicated language, but it's perfectly correct. Conrad's books, written in his third language, are in a difficult, seemingly disjointed style, but his stream-of-consciousness prose always has lexical precision, something he worked on meticulously.

Nabokov, also trilingual, is considered one of the leading prose stylists of the 20th century and his fiction is characterized by linguistic playfulness. Nabokov paid extra attention to perfecting his beautiful prose.

F*ollow these two grand authors' example and check, check, and recheck your text.*

Naturally, neither Conrad nor Nabokov did all this work to perfect their texts alone. They, like all authors, used friends and family as first readers, and editors and proofreaders to improve their writing. Today's authors have the additional benefit of the internet. There are many tools online that can help you with your writing. Turn to the next chapter.

6

ONLINE TOOLS

Writing in another language is so much easier today than it was when I started out. Or when Conrad and Nabokov worked on their manuscripts. I know this next statement is going to age me, but there were none of these resources when I began thinking about writing as a serious career choice in 2003.

Online Dictionaries

When I enrolled on the MA in Creative Writing course some fifteen years ago, my lovely husband, the original Englishman, bought me a Collins dictionary and a thesaurus. These huge tomes are still on my shelf, and occasionally I refer to them, but for the most part I now rely on resources online. The thesaurus and dictionary pages are always open on my desktop.

I also use *Grammarly*, a useful software tool that corrects your language as you write. It also allows you to choose whether you write in American or British English, and gives a reason for any changes it offers as you type.

Using *Grammarly* has increased my confidence online enormously. Writing blogs, social media posts, and articles is so much easier when you have software to correct your work. With *Word* and *Scrivener*, which I am using to write this book, I rely on their own correction tools. I find that the grammar check in *Word* can be tricky when switching languages, but if I keep to one language when writing, it works well.

There are several online sites dedicated to English grammar too. As an example, I used to struggle to know in which order to place adjectives until I found this useful list online:

1. **Quantity** (e.g. one, many)
2. **Value/Opinion** (e.g. wonderful, awful)
3. **Size** (e.g. little, broad)
4. **Age** (e.g. new, six-year-old)
5. **Physical Quality** (e.g. oval, rough)
6. **Color** (e.g. red, bright)
7. **Origin/Nationality** (e.g. English, Chinese)
8. **Material** (e.g. wool, metal)
9. **Type/Purpose** (e.g. riding, running)

Word Lists

In addition to online dictionaries and grammar aides, there are useful lists of words and phrases connected to particular situations, such as love scenes, or physical states, such as excitement or happiness. There are even eye-color charts.

Recently, when writing a scene where a body was

found on a beach, I realized I knew nothing about forensics. I went online and found a site describing the various stages of a body's decomposition in sea water.

You can find lists on almost any specialist subject online. Sites such as *Pinterest*, *Goodreads*, even *FaceBook* and *Instagram* as well as many, many blogs will give you ideas on word choices. Sometimes just typing a word or a phrase that you're not sure about into *Google* will show you the correct usage of the word.

Beware, however. Always make sure the site is authentic and its expertise verified either by a recognized association or authority.

Writing Blogs

There is a plethora of writing advice online too. I follow many writing blogs and vlogs. (A note: I do not have any association with any of the recommended pieces of software or sites quoted in this book.) Here are some writing sites that I read regularly:

The Write Life

Writer's Digest

The Write Practice

The Creative Penn

Daily Writing Tips

Better Novel Project

Well-Storied

Jane Friedman

Orna Ross

Reedsy

Selfpublishing Formula

NaNoWriMo

7

FIRST READERS

When I started writing fiction, I struggled to show my work to anyone at all. But when I enrolled on an MA in Creative Writing that had to change. There were weekly critique sessions when everyone had to read their work out loud, so I had to get used to it. During those sessions, I found that my text stood out for its original voice, but also for the expressions I used. Some were unique (good), but some were just incorrect expressions, colloquialisms, metaphors, or similes. I also had a habit of getting the prepositions wrong. (And I still do—we don't have any of those in Finnish.)

My first experience of showing my writing to

someone new was a dramatic and painful experience (see Chapter 2) but slowly, I got used to it.

When I got to know other writers, I came to realize that their work was not as perfect as I originally thought, even when it was written in their mother tongue.

Some Home Truths About Writers

This is what I found out about other writers when I had worked in the industry for a few years.

1. Every writer, however famous or experienced, needs his or her work edited.

2. Most writers have a valued first reader, be it editor or friend, a fellow writer or a partner. Many famous authors show their work to their partners first before letting anyone else see it.

3. The first manuscript is just a shadow of the finished product that the readers will see. There will be several edits made by the author. By the time an editor gets involved, the writer thinks the book is already perfect, only to find the text littered with red marks when it is returned. However many times I go through this process, I am always surprised (although less gutted nowadays) at the sheer number of corrections. (We never learn.)

4. The acknowledgements at the back of novels, or any book for that matter, often have a long list of people whom the author thanks. These are ALL first, second, third, or twentieth readers. Today many authors have whole teams of so-called Beta Readers, who go through the text and note discrepancies that even the professional editor and proofreader have missed.

5. Most published books have one or two mistakes. Yes, I know, this may come as a shock to you, but just look carefully at any book and you will spot a spelling mistake, a missing comma, even a factual error. This doesn't make it right or excusable, but just shows that the editing process has no end. With digitalization and print on demand production, it's now easier to upload several corrected copies of a book.

. . .

Use a Native Reader

As an author writing in another language, your first reader should ideally be a native speaker. You should also use several first readers as well as professional editors to iron out problems and to get feedback on your manuscript.

Your first native reader can be anybody, but I do find it easier to work with the same person on all of my books. Over the years the first reader gets to know your style, recognizes the phrases that are unique to you, and is able to tell what you mean by them.

It's important that the first reader understands what you are trying to say with your words. It might, therefore, be a good idea to give them an outline of the subject or plot before you give them the whole manuscript.

It may be easier if the first reader knows you but,

of course, it is not necessary. Very much like working with a translator, you don't even have to be in the same country. The important thing is that she or he gets to know your work and your writing style.

If you are struggling to find someone to look over your work, there are several online services you can use. The Alliance of Independent Authors, for example, has a list of several vetted services for authors. Make sure any readers come with good recommendations and that you feel comfortable working with them.

Blogging

Of course, the more you write in another language, the better you will become at it. When I first started thinking about a writing career, I began a weekly blog. The discipline of having to produce a coherent piece of writing once a week gave me a good writing routine and helped me overcome my shyness about other people seeing my work. The blog was also a very good way to find other writers as well as Beta (or first) Readers.

Blogging features strongly in my book *Turn Your Story Into Fiction in 10 Easy Steps* because it was on my blog that I first began telling the story of how I met and married my Englishman. Those blogposts gave birth to my first published novel, *The English Heart.* I talk more about blogging in Chapter 10.

8

EXPERTS AND RESEARCH

Research and using expert advice is important for any writer, but for the author who writes in another language it's even more vital that you know the correct terminology, slang, or common expressions for any given subject.

When I was writing *The Nordic Heart* series, in which one of the main characters is in the Royal Navy, I needed to sound as if I was born to that world and knew the ins and outs of a military ship, including the weaponry and control systems. I also needed to know the terms Navy wives used and also the "Jackspeak" on board ships and submarines. About 30 percent of the novels are written from the male protagonist's point of view, so I also needed to sound as if I'd served in the Royal Navy.

I was lucky in that my first reader had also been in the Navy, so he could point out some of the mistakes I'd made, but I also asked another expert to give the manuscript a final read. As I wrote more books in the series, and moved into areas that my first reader had never experienced, such as serving in a Polaris nuclear submarine, I had to rely more and more on my second Navy expert.

The military have the strangest nicknames for everyday items as well as the specific equipment they use and the different ranks and duties. The British Navy, for example, has weird names for food on ships and submarines. For example, "arrigones" are tinned tomatoes. This hails from the days when one of the suppliers of Italian tinned tomatoes was Signor A. Riggoni, a name emblazoned on the labels. "Babies' Heads," on the other hand, is steak-and-kidney pudding.

One of my main sources of such colloquialisms was a book called *Jackspeak: The Pusser's Rum Guide to Royal Navy Slanguage*. This, essentially a joke book, was given to my husband (who served in the Royal Navy as a submarine officer) several years ago for his amusement. For me, this book was like a small thesaurus.

"But surely you can find all this stuff online?" you ask. Yes, some of it, but the above mentioned book isn't in an eBook format, and trying to find similar information about the British Navy has proved very difficult. I have found some sites aimed at staff who've served on a specific ship or submarine which have been useful, but for the most part the Royal Navy is very secretive.

You may be writing about a similarly difficult subject, in which case it's vital to find experts who can help you with your research.

At the moment I am writing a second novel set in the Åland Islands and I need to know a lot about seafaring there, such as the different parts of a sailing boat, a ferry, and a motorboat. I also need to know how a newspaper office works on the Islands and how the police force functions there. I can find all of this online, especially as I can read the information in Swedish. This is another benefit of writing in another language. You are able find information that isn't always translated into another language.

If you are using a second or third language, research is particularly important, even when writing about matters you know intimately. I was a Navy wife for many years, but you'd be amazed how many times my naval expert corrected some small thing that no one but those who have been in the Navy would know. One such correction was the use of the definite article in a term used for naval housing. I'd written "the married quarters" and he said it's either "the married quarter" or "married quarters." Never "the married quarters." You may think this is splitting hairs, but remember what I said about not making the reader stop in their tracks? How even a small error will make readers who spot it leave the world that you have created? Suddenly, puff, such readers are thinking about the writer and the writing rather than the story or world you have created.

My recommendation is to find an expert for any part of your manuscript that requires specific terminology, but as well as experts, it's important for a professional editor to have the final say in the language you use.

9

EDITING AND PROOFREADING

After you've finished your manuscript, given it to a native reader and several other readers, be they your Beta Readers, or experts in the particular field, and looked through your work, you need to employ a professional editor. Employing an editor has many, many benefits.

Firstly, you get an unbiased, professional opinion of your manuscript. As well as the actual language, including spelling mistakes, wrong prepositions, correcting the tense, the order of the adjectives, and so on, an editor will also line edit the work.

There are three kinds of editing, depending on the stage of your manuscript. If, like me, you use a wide range of readers, including a native speaker, Beta Readers and experts, you probably don't need to use every type of editor.

However, if this is your first book, I'd spend as much as you can afford on editing the work. You've invested a lot of time on the manuscript, why not make it the best it possibly can be?

Readers are not forgiving; they will spot any mistake or problem with the plot or characters. Robert McKee, the Hollywood script-writing guru says: "The audience is not only amazingly sensitive, but as it settles into a darkened theater its collective IQ jumps twenty-five points." (Robert McKee, *Story*, Methuen Publishing 1999).

The same is true about readers. As soon as they start reading your book, they become your harshest critic and your most avid reader in one. Within the first sentences, a contract forms between you, the writer, and the reader. The reader agrees to accept and enjoy the story, the world you have created, and you agree to give them this enjoyment. You as a writer must therefore make sure you do everything in your power to help the reader to suspend disbelief.

Mistakes in the language, plot, point of view, tense, and so on will break this contract with readers and they will stop reading your book, or worse, write an unfavorable review. Which is harsh, I know.

Before I go on, I must make the point that you cannot please all the people all of the time. Negative reviews happen, however well you have prepared your book for publication. They happen to all writers, be they famous, traditionally published authors, or first-time indie writers.

Some say that one-star reviews give your book authenticity. If all your reviews are glowing, it is doubtful they are all genuine. Are they honest and true reviews, or just your friends who've read your book and want to help you along in your new career? These friends and family will want you to succeed, so they may have their blinkers on. Having a few unfavorable reviews shows potential readers that the book has been read widely, not just by those who know the author.

To insure yourself against too many unfavorable reviews, or readers who never get to the end of your book, you must employ a professional editor AND proofreader. And I mean a *professional* editor. As good as your mum, dad, or partner are as first readers, they should not be your editors. It's OK to use people close to you as Beta Readers, or experts in their field, but they mustn't take the place of an editor. Ideally, your editor is a stranger, or someone with whom you have a professional relationship. There are several different kinds of editors and editing.

The Developmental Edit

The first edit is often called the Developmental

Edit, also called "substantive edit," looks at the major structural issues in a book. Instead of suggesting that an individual sentence is wrong, or a particular scene could be shorter, the editor might suggest wholesale changes to the book that will involve significant rewriting.

A developmental edit concerns itself mainly with the plot, the characterization, and setting of the manuscript. Could a plot line be added or removed? Could a character be added or removed to help the story move along? Could a passage of prose be turned into dialogue? Does the book have too much backstory, or not enough? Does the manuscript follow the Five Commandments of Storytelling? (See below)

As you become more used to storytelling, you will find that your need for a developmental edit diminishes. Writing improves your craft and you are able to spot many of the issues yourself before you even give the book to your first reader.

There is a lot of advice on how to construct a

story online. Many people have quoted the Five Commandments of Storytelling but here's my take on them.

Five Commandments of Storytelling

1. Inciting Incident

Something has to happen to the protagonist to change his world. For example, a woman who's never been in love meets the man of her dreams when she bumps into him in a park. Perhaps she accidentally pours hot coffee over his pristine, white shirt.

2. Progressive Complications

Complications are crucial in a story, and it's also important that the problems mount up—ie become progressive. For example, the man of her dreams (whose shirt she ruined) is a single dad with three kids. Then she finds out his wife died and he cannot love anyone else as much. And his kids hate him dating anyone else.

3. Crisis

This is the point where our heroine is forced to

act. Will she forget about this man she loves and who loves her back? There has to be something, like a job offer on the other side of the world, a discovery that the wife is alive after all, or something to force our loved-up protagonists to act.

4. Climax

This is where the characters make the final decision and act on it. She moves away and tries to forget about our man or the wife turns out to be a cheating tramp, who, all of this time, has lived a second life with another man on a desert island in the middle of the South Seas.

5. Resolution

This is where all the threads of the main plot and the side plots are brought together and the book ends. Our couple get together and marry, and the born-again wife ends up alone.

A word of warning, however. The above example is a very simplistic way of looking at a story, or a novel. I agree with the Nobel-prize winning author, Doris Lessing, who said,

> *There are no laws for the novel. There have never been, nor can there ever be.*

When I was writing my first book, *Coffee and Vodka*, I was able to use my fellow students and tutors on my MA course to comment on the plot and characterizations in the novel. I learned a huge amount about how to tell a story and what to include and remove in the plot. I also began to understand the strengths and weaknesses in my particular writing style. It was during that year that I decided to set my books in the Nordic countries, because I knew that this is something particular to me: to be able to tell a story in English set in Finland or Sweden.

Since the course, I have used several other author friends, as well as my Beta Readers, to carry out this stage of editing. My editor, who mainly does the line edit (see below), also sometimes suggests some major changes, but this is less common now that I've written and published nine fiction titles. I believe strongly that the more you write the better you become.

. . .

The Line Edit

A Line Edit usually follows the developmental edit. Here the editor looks exclusively at the more linguistic areas of the manuscript. These may include the use of clichés, adverbs, filter words, point of view or tense.

A line edit addresses the creative content, writing style, and language use at sentence and paragraph level. But the purpose of a line edit is not to comb the manuscript for errors—rather, a line edit focuses on the way you use language to communicate your story to the reader.

This phase of editing is very important to authors who write in another language. It is at this stage that the editor will pick up the quirkiness of your language use. She will suggest alternatives to expressions that you may have transposed from your native tongue. Sometimes, these "new" expressions are justified, especially if the protagonist is also a non-native speaker. However, it's important that the reader understands what is meant by the unusual language, and here a line editor can advise you.

In *The Nordic Heart* series I use many naval expressions, which my line editor didn't know. Whenever she queried one of these, I went back to my Navy expert (see previous chapter) and confirmed the correct usage of the term or phrase.

I remember vividly the day my first novel, *Coffee and Vodka*, was assessed by one of the professors on my MA in Creative Writing. The professor congratulated me on making the book sound as if the protagonist were non-English speakers without making it sound strange, or wrong. "I'm not sure if you did that consciously or unconsciously," he added.

I couldn't say if I had or hadn't. All the main characters in that book are from Finland and I'd spent months with them in my head, so I would have consciously made them sound Finnish. *Coffee and Vodka* was subsequently professionally edited, but I did make sure that none of the "Finnishisms" were taken out. Funnily enough, this novel is still selling well and many people have told me it's their favorite book of mine.

The Copy Edit

The last stage of editing is the Copy Edit. It's the final check of the language used in the book and involves grammar, punctuation, spelling, but also changes to words, word order, sentence length, and appearance. It may even include the restructuring or re-ordering of paragraphs.

Although I do recommend that you employ a professional to do a developmental and a line edit, if your funds do not stretch to every stage, this is one you *absolutely cannot skip*. You can use Beta Readers, friends, fellow writers, or even family to comment on your manuscript and let you know if there are any issues with plot or characters, but you cannot use a person who is not a professional editor to do your copy edit. *I cannot emphasize this enough.*

American v British Spelling

If you write in English, I wanted to say a word about American versus British spelling. When I started writing, I automatically began using British spelling, mainly because I was living in the UK and it seemed natural.

When I worked for the BBC, it was considered almost a crime to use American spelling, so I carefully removed any words that even hinted toward American use of the language.

However, in my last book, which is set in the Åland Islands, I used American spelling, mainly because the book is set entirely on the Islands, and only a few scenes are set in Britain. I also wanted to appeal to a wider audience.

But there are two important considerations when choosing which regional language to use.

. . .

1. Be consistent

If you use American spelling, make sure it's used throughout the book (and a series). *The Nordic Heart* series, which tells the story of Peter, a Royal Navy officer, and Kaisa, his Finnish girlfriend, uses British spelling throughout. It would have seemed strange for my characters to speak "American" when Peter is a serving British Navy officer, and therefore very patriotic and proud of his country. Which brings me to the second point.

2. Make sure the language suits the story

If you are writing a fantasy book, I'd use American spelling because there are no reference points to the real world. (Unless the book is a dystopian novel set in the UK.) If, however, you (like me in my series) are telling a story set in the UK, it would be wrong to use American words and expressions unless the protagonist is from the US. You see how this works?

The reason many writers would like to use American English is that the book-buying market is much larger in the US than it is in the UK. There are some 325 million people living in the United States compared to "just" 66 million in Britain. The numbers speak for themselves.

Even though I use British spelling across most of my books, half my sales come from the US, Canada, and Australia, so using one particular regional language doesn't mean cutting out the rest of the world. But using US spelling may make your books more popular in North America. Both Canada and Australia, the latter in particular, have their own vocabulary and colloquialisms. These are not, however, commonly used by authors who live outside these two countries.

In summary, use the dialect or spelling of the protagonist. Not only will it sound authentic to the readers, but it will also make your characters realistic. It will give them a unique personality.

The Proofread

The proofread is the final look at the manuscript

as a novel. This often takes into account the formatting of the book, how the pages, paragraphs and headings are organized, whether they are consistent throughout the book or not. For example, are capital letters and italics used consistently? Is the text in the right place, ie are the size of the margins the same across the book? Finally, the proof editor should pick up any minor errors that might have been overlooked by the copy editor.

As you can see, even after you have completed your work on the manuscript, there is still much to be done before you can send it to the printers or publish it online as an eBook. Furthermore as an indie author, I know that having a well-edited, clean copy of my book, with a story that keeps the readers' attention and characters who are complicated and authentic, is just the entry fee to the publishing marketplace.

As an author in another language, your strengths are in your unique storytelling. You can take the reader to places they may not have heard of, let alone experienced. Equally, you can create characters who are different and intriguing. But, you have to work a little harder to make sure your language is faultless, while still being particular to you. Employing professionals to help you achieve this clean copy is vital.

10

DEVELOPING YOUR WRITING SKILLS

All writers, not just those who are writing in a "foreign" language are constantly, consciously developing their writing skills. I've never yet met a writer who is totally happy with their latest book. We all know we develop as we become more experienced. Writing, like any form of art, is a craft: you need to sharpen your tools to become a better author.

The Importance of Reading

Writers have the wonderful ability to examine other authors' work closely. We can analyze how other authors in our genre write. We can learn from how they use language; the way they tell a story; how they describe characters, handle the back story, or use dialogue to bring the story forward. In the privacy of our homes, or in a classroom, or coffee shop, we can study any piece of writing and take useful lessons from it. In other words, we can read and learn.

I consume a huge number of books in a year. These are mainly novels and mostly in my genre in English, because that is where I learn most. I read British and American books, with a few Canadian and Australian fiction titles thrown in for good measure. I also read quite a few translated novels, especially from the Nordic region. Again, this is so that I can learn from authors who hail from my part of the world as well as those from the UK, where I now live. I love the fact that reading novels is now part of my job!

I was afraid that taking my MA in Creative Writing would spoil reading for me, because I'd be looking at books in a professional way rather than simply enjoying them. I thought I'd be noting the way the author has dealt with a certain tricky piece of back story, or "showing" rather than "telling" a person's race, for example. To an extent this was a justified fear, because I cannot ignore technical issues, like the slapdash use of point of view, or the writer revealing too much of a character's history too quickly. But this is balanced by the pure joy when I find a book that is perfect (or almost perfect—I am really, really hard to please, as all authors are I'm sure).

It's incredibly satisfying when you spot a beautiful expression, or a way to portray the character's peculiarities in just one word. When I find something I like, I note it down, or highlight the section on my Kindle. When lacking inspiration while writing, I go back to these notes, and often find something that triggers a breakthrough in my own writing. (Note: I'm not talking about plagiarism—never, ever, copy any other authors' words. Rather learn from *how* they write.)

This happened recently when I read *Little Fires Everywhere*, by Celeste Ng. When describing the tenant Mia Pearl, a single mother, the author reveals just as much about the character of the landlord, Mrs Richardson, and her family. Using an omniscient point of view, the author recounts how the Richardson family first saw Mia Pearl:

> *They noticed that she wore no ring on her left hand, though she wore plenty of other rings: a big amethyst on her first finger, one made from silver spoon handle on her pinkie, and one on her thumb that to Mrs. Richardson looked suspiciously like a mood ring. (Little Fires Everywhere* by Celeste Ng)

The word "suspiciously" tells the reader much about Mrs Richardson's character.

Eavesdropping

All writers love people-watching and listening to other people's conversations. As a writer in another language, this kind of eaves-dropping is even more vital. When on a bus, train, street, in a cafe, or even the gym, listen in on conversations and note down words and expressions that you find new or interesting. Think about what would be the equivalent in your own language. This will help you remember them when you come to write.

Don't, however, try to use direct translations of your own in your text. It's very rare that expressions transfer easily between languages and cultures. I've tried many a time to get such expressions past my first readers and editors. Unless, of course, your character speaks English as a second language and he or she uses a phrase wrongly. In this case, you are describing the character through the language he or she uses.

Marina Lewycka adopts this method very effectively in her writing, especially in her novel *A Short History of Tractors in Ukrainian*. Check this author out; she is brilliant at describing displacement and characters from different cultures trying to communicate.

Write, Write, and Write More

The more you write in another language the better at it you will become. This is why I started my blog in 2007. I needed the discipline of turning out a blog post each week. The blog, which was titled *Helena's London Life,* is now on my website (www.helenahalme.com/blog) and although the blogging is rather different now, I still try to write a post at least once every month. The first blog gave birth to my most successful novel, *The English Heart*, so I will forever be grateful for that. (More about blogging below.)

It's also useful to find a time of day when your creative juices are flowing more freely. Many authors I know write in the mornings, but you may not be a morning person. Some writers like to burn the midnight oil—if you have a young family, this might be the only time you are able to concentrate on your story.

I try to write first thing in the morning. My brain is fresh and I am able to concentrate on the project properly. If I haven't been able to write in the morning, I get down to the manuscript sometime during the day. I have a daily word target (see below), or if editing, a certain number of chapters I need to complete.

Many people think that authors write when they

feel the presence of the writing muse. I was one of those people before I took my MA in Creative Writing. I soon realized that writing is like any other job—you just have to get down to it and complete the day's tasks.

Be Disciplined

One of the questions I am asked quite frequently is whether I write every day and how many words I produce during each writing session.

For me, my daily target is to write at least 500 words five days a week. Most weekdays I manage to write 1,500 to 2,000 words, and sometime more than this. I have noticed, however, that if I write 3,000 words or more, I struggle to write the following day. So, personally, I have to control my urge to write too much. This may sound crazy to a new writer, but you learn as you go along. My method has developed over the last fifteen years, or so, since I've been writing professionally.

Discipline is hugely important to me, and to many

of the successful writers I know. As I said before, this is my job. What kind of writer would I be if I didn't write every working day?

Over the years, I have learned that discipline cuts both ways. It's important not to overdo it. Even if I am on a deadline, I take weekends off to rest my mind and body. This pays off on Monday, when 2,000 words flow quickly and (almost) painlessly.

Holidays are equally sacred to me, although I do find that I need to get some words down after about four days. If I do this, I can carry on having a rest. I don't really go anywhere without taking my laptop!

Your Mind Is a Treasure Trove

I find that when I am away from my normal surroundings, new plot ideas often come into my head and I just have to get them down. The mind is a treasure trove, so treat it as such and note down your ideas wherever and whenever they occur, even writing a few chapters of the story. I don't think I've been on a holiday in the past fifteen years without plotting a new novel set in that location.

My drawer contains unfinished novels set in California, Phoenix, Provence, Lisbon, Barcelona, Madrid, Southern Spain, Puglia and Rome, Paris and, of course, many of the cities in Finland and Sweden, such as Tampere, Stockholm, Luleå—and Lapland. One of these days I shall rekindle those love affairs and finish those manuscripts one by one! (See below where I compare writing a new book to embarking on a new relationship.)

The most important thing is to learn your own strengths and weaknesses when it comes to getting the words out. When are you most productive, when does your adopted language flow, when do you need to take a break, how do your energy levels change? Naturally, the more you write, the more you can write and the more polished the text.

Write a Regular Blog

As well as providing a useful discipline, blogging is an excellent way to hone your writing skills.

When I had finished my MA in Creative Writing, I found it hard to keep the writing going every day without the weekly critique sessions provided on the course. This was until I discovered blogging.

I've been blogging since 2007 and my first blog gave birth to my first book in *The Nordic Heart* series. I'd been writing a weekly blog post for a few months, and been making friends in the blogosphere through the Blogger platform, when several of my readers asked me why I'd move to the UK.

I began a series called, *How I Came to Be in England*, telling the story of how I met my husband, a Royal Navy officer, at the British Embassy in Helsinki (The Inciting Incident). The blog described the difficulties of such a love affair, including the fact that I lived in a country friendly to the Soviet Union and had a father who disapproved of foreigners (Progressive Complications and Crisis), and how we eventually had to marry hastily in Portsmouth due to red tape (Climax), only to go through a second, proper wedding in Finland and live happily ever after (Resolution).

After many, many edits including changing the point of view from first person to third, and inventing new characters and removing others, this story of how I came to be in England eventually became *The English Heart.* Although my blog posts gave birth to a novel, blogging is very different from writing a piece of fiction. Blogs generally either have a chatty style, or they are informative posts about subjects such as writing fiction or marketing a book. It's also important to consider keywords and online rankings when writing a blog, something that affects the style of writing.

When I began blogging, it was quite common to

use the platform to write a book. Nowadays, however, if you want to develop a story with the help of online readership, there are sites such as *Wattpad*, where writers can upload chapters of their current manuscript for feedback from a wide readership. Some of the authors who have generated a buzz on *Wattpad* have gone on to sign book deals or their stories have been opted for TV series or films. If, however, blogging is your thing and you want your website to have a large audience, here are a few tips on writing a blog post in another language.

1. Plan the subject and main points

Plan the blog before you start writing. Just jot down the main points and make those your first, tentative chapter headings. I tend to have a notepad next to my laptop and write down up to ten points I want to make in the blog post I am writing.

2. Write the first draft quickly

Using your main points, just get your thoughts onto the blog, or on any writing software you're using (*Scrivener* or *Word*, for example). I write a blog in a matter of minutes and then edit it for up to two hours. I know this sounds like a long time, but as I said earlier, I consider it important to turn out a clean copy of any text I publish.

3. Correct your work

Go through the words with a fine toothcomb. Remove any unnecessary sentences or headings. Use any widgets you have to make the post visible online with chapter headings, keywords, and other Search Engine Optimization tools.

4. Go and make a cup of coffee

This is the point where you need to get some distance from your writing. If you can leave it for a longer period, so much the better. You will notice mistakes, often after your brain has had a chance to think about something else.

5. Read out loud

If your spoken language is stronger than your written one (which is often the case when using a language that is not your mother tongue), reading your text out loud will reveal mistakes that you wouldn't have otherwise noticed. I use this method even in my novel writing, in addition to letting the manuscript "stew" for a few weeks or even months.

Beware the Inner Critic

I have emphasized in the previous chapters the importance of checking and rechecking your work. I've also discussed using online tools to help you write in grammatically correct language without spelling mistakes, as well as using native speakers as first readers. Doing your research and seeking help from experts to ensure you are employing the correct terminology is also vital. Using a professional editor is by far the most important step in ensuring your language is polished and will not be "noticed" by the reader, thus allowing them to suspend disbelief and enjoy your story, blog, or nonfiction title.

I've also recommended that you read other books to learn from authors writing in the language you're planning to use, as well as write as much as you can in that language.

BUT

It is also very important that you do not let other authors' words or all the technical issues with language stop you from writing.

Writing Is a Creative Process

Writing is a creative process that needs an open, positive mind. You need to be confident that you can produce the right words and sentences to describe a series of events and make up an engaging story for your readers to enjoy.

Writers often talk about the compulsion to write, a need to get a story that's buzzing in their head out. I often get asked if I enjoy writing. Even after all the years that I have been writing—first through keeping a diary, then blogging, then tentatively writing a novel, and now publishing new work regularly—I still don't have a satisfactory answer to this question.

I love being able to do what I've always wanted to do: write stories that people, readers, like to read. But the writing process is far from pleasurable.

And even that statement isn't right. The moment you know you've started a new story and the road ahead of you lies open is blissful. You know anything could happen to these characters—even if you've worked out a tight plot for them—and you cannot wait to put it all down on paper (or tap it into your computer).

I compare this initial euphoria of starting a story to the feelings you get when you first fall in love or are infatuated by a new person in your life.

A Love Affair

I often describe writing a book as having a love affair. In the first heady moments when you've met someone new, you are infatuated with them. You love everything about them, their smile, their laughter, their quirky expressions, even their smelly feet or their annoying habit of slurping the milk with their muesli in the morning. It's the same with my new book. I love the new plot, the new characters, the new setting. I cannot wait to get back to the story and write more of it.

Then I have a lover's tiff—the first, devastating argument when I realize my new love is just a normal human being. A hugely annoying human at that!

Somewhere in the middle of the new novel, when I've got stuck with the plot, or some new scenes have crept in that really don't work, or I notice a major hole in the storyline, all I want to do is give up.

And sometimes, that's exactly what I do. I have several unfinished manuscripts in my virtual desk drawer. Unfinished stories that just didn't make it past the 30,000 word point. Even though these stories don't run the course, I still think about them. One day, I will go back to them and make them work. To me, these unfinished stories are both useful exercises in the craft of writing and a future resource that can be turned into a fully-fledged novel.

The next phase—if the story runs the course—is

the happiness I feel when I have been able to fix the plot, or turn the characters around so that they work for the novel. Once I've got past the major arch of the story I am literally on the downhill ride. I can lift my legs off the pedals and just let that bicycle carry me down for the rest of the book. This is when my relationship with my writing is working; I turn up in the morning, write my 2,000 words, and let the story be until I see it again the next day.

When I know I've written the last sentence, the rapture I feel is indescribable. It's as if I've given birth to something wonderful and new! I know I need to let my first reader have the manuscript, and I know he will have a lot of corrections to make, and ideas about the structure and the characters, but at least I have something for him to read. And I know that the editing process will be long, possibly even longer than the time I've spent writing the novel. But I know I have 70,000 or so words on a page that can be corrected. I have something to show for all the hours I've spent typing away at the laptop, emptying my mind and creating a story.

You cannot edit an empty page

Try not to let your inner critic of your use of a non-native language stop your flow. Remember that the first draft of your manuscript, whether you are a native speaker or not, is just that—a draft. Everyone has their work corrected, so write freely. It's the meaning of the words, as well as the language, that is important. Remember what I said in Chapter 7. All writers use several first readers, editors, and proofreaders to give feedback and correct their work.

Only you can write that book!

You can edit the book until the cows come home, but if you haven't written anything there will be nothing to edit.

WRITERS WHO WRITE IN ANOTHER LANGUAGE

When writing this guide, I wanted to include the views of other authors who write in a language that is not their mother tongue. I posed three questions to each of the authors:

1. *Why do you write in English?*
2. *How does writing in another language influence your work? Or does it? Is there a difference?*
3. *What advice would you give to an author who would like to write in a second (or even third or fourth) language?*

Heidi Amsinck

Heidi Amsinck, a writer and journalist born in Copenhagen, spent many years covering Britain for the Danish press, including a spell as London Correspondent for the broadsheet daily Jyllands-Posten. *She has written numerous short stories for radio including* Copenhagen Confidential *and* Copenhagen Curios, *the three-story sets of Danish Noir produced by Sweet Talk for BBC Radio 4. A graduate of the MA in Creative Writing at Birkbeck, University of London, Heidi lives in Surrey, in the UK. She was previously shortlisted for the V.S. Pritchett Memorial Prize.* Last Train to Helsingor *is her first published collection of stories.*

1. Why do you write in English?

I never made a conscious decision to do so. It just happened. I wanted to tell dark and ghostly stories about Copenhagen and Denmark to my family and friends here in the UK, and as I speak English with them, I guess it came naturally.

2. How does writing in another language influence your work? Or does it? Is there a difference?

There is a huge difference. Especially when, like me, you are writing about home. Doing so in a second language is like wearing a pair of spectacles that allows you to notice the "otherness" of the familiar. You have to work harder to find the right words, and sometimes you make mistakes, but if you're lucky, your prose feels fresh with just a tinge of the unusual.

I only ever wrote one short story in Danish and hated its earnest ordinariness.

3. What advice would you give to an author who would like to write in a second (or even third or fourth) language?

To write successfully in another language, I believe you have to inhabit it. English is the language I speak with my children and closest friends, so I have a deep emotional connection with it. I live and breathe English. My diary is in English, as are my notebooks. The other piece of advice I'd give to all aspiring writers–and in particularly those writing in English as their second language—is to read ferociously and to listen to original works of fiction on Radio 4 as often as you can. When I arrived in the UK in 1992, someone told me to listen to *The Archers* every night in order to improve my English (unintentionally sparking a lifelong obsession with the "everyday story of country folk," but that is a different story).

If you want to go all out, and prove your English writing prowess, I'd recommend an MA in Creative Writing. I took one at Birkbeck, University of London, and it was there that I began to take myself seriously as a writer. A writer who just happens to write in English.

Freddie P. Peters

Freddie P. Peters lives in North London. A Law graduate from The Sorbonne-Paris and King's College London, she started her career as a lawyer (oops) and then became an investment banker (gulp). Twenty-five years spent in the Square Mile (City of London) working for too-big-

to-fail international banks did give her a view on many hot topics from financial crises to being foreign and female in a male-dominated industry, and from contemporary art to politics, without forgetting the most essential of questions "Where have ethics gone in all of this?".

When she is not writing, Freddie devotes her time to supporting young artists and small art galleries or mentoring students and young professionals.

Collapse *is the first financial and espionage thriller in the Henry Crowne: Paying the Price trilogy. You can find Freddie easily at www.freddiep-peters.com for more insight into the books' background stories. Freddie is also on Facebook at Freddieppeters.Author.*

1. Why Do You Write in English?

Thirty-two years in the UK is a very long time… but time is not everything. I came to the UK to delve into its culture. I worked almost exclusively in English-speaking companies and never sought the comfort of South Kensington's French enclave. I moved to London to experience London fully as a foreigner, then as a Londoner. It made me.

So many years of life, work and culture have shaped my way of thinking, feeling, and expressing. I can't imagine writing in any language other than English. Writing in French, which I sometimes still do, feels wooden, somewhat imprecise, not quite in sync with what I am trying to convey.

My French friends say it too—You are so "*Englocized.*" To be frank, I can't point to what makes me so, but I understand what they are getting at, a feeling of closeness and yet not quite belonging. English helps me express this sentiment and I enjoy exploring its effect on my writing.

2. How does writing in another language influence your work? Or does it? Is there a difference?

Despite what I have previously said, writing in English was a challenge. To start with, there was a disconnect I did not expect between wanting and doing. I was accustomed to the language of business, comfortable with its formulation. There was always some work to be done to arrive at a finished, even polished product but in the end it was always fluent.

Writing fiction made me regress back to writing English with a French language construction. It was a disquieting experience to begin with, then thrilling when I was able to spot the old French patterns and work around them.

My style has become clearer because I had to think so much more about it, never taking it for granted the way a native speaker might. I select words carefully to make sure they are *right.* It's a craft. Perhaps akin to chiseling or carving a sculpture. Precise, beautiful, and powerful.

3. What advice would you give an author who would like to write in a second (or even third or fourth) language?

I have three recommendations:

1. Read a lot in the language in which you want to write, to give yourself the spectrum, the richness, and the awareness of that language.

2. Decide whether you don't mind sounding

foreign... it may suit the storyline, the characters etc.

3. If you decide to immerse yourself completely in your chosen language, and want to sound authentic, get a good trusted editor who can help you develop your own style in that language. But *not* someone who seeks to rewrite the story in your place (there are many of them around, and they also charge a fortune!)

Eivor Martinus

Eivor was born in Sweden and moved to England on marrying theater and TV director Derek Martinus in the 1960s. She has a degree in English and Swedish literature from the universities of Lund and Gothenburg, Sweden. Since the sixties she has published articles, essays, short stories, novels, plays, translations, two biographies, and two autobiographical works.

To date she has translated fifteen plays by August Strindberg, twelve of which have been published and performed in England and/or the USA.

1. Why do you write in English?

I moved to England more than fifty years ago, so I have spent most of my life there. English gradually took root in me and today I am equally happy writing in Swedish or English.

I alternate between English and Swedish. The first piece I wrote in English was a play, which was performed at a small theater in London. I had lived in England for over ten years at the time and I had published my first adult novel in Swedish, but it seemed natural to write that particular play in English since it was about theater people in London, something I was familiar with. My experience in that field was purely in English.

After that I wrote four novels in Swedish in the youth fiction category and then spent about twenty years translating and adapting novels and plays into both languages.

In the last ten years I have returned to my mother tongue and have published four books in Sweden. For me, the topic determines whether I write in English or Swedish. It helps to have a sympathetic Swedish publisher, of course.

2. How does writing in another language influence your work or does it?

Is there a difference?

I think I am more cautious when I write in English. I tread carefully and examine each paragraph more critically than when I write in Swedish. I take more liberties with the language in Swedish, but I never seem to mix the two languages. I have always made a conscious effort to keep them apart and make sure I don't end up with two half languages. They exist side by side. I put the one I am not using away to avoid "translating" while writing. For me, it is essential to keep the two languages separate and to keep reading extensively in both languages. I always have at least two books in both languages by my bed and I subscribe to three Swedish newspapers to keep up to date and to counteract the powerful presence of English in the media.

3. What advice would you give to an author who would like to write in a second or even a third or fourth language?

Don't underestimate the problems and don't overestimate your knowledge of the languages. Read as much as you can in the language that is not your mother tongue—or best language. Make sure you listen to people and if possible to radio programs or lectures in your second language.

I took a degree in English literature with an emphasis on literature before 1800. I also studied Swedish literature (including world literature) at a Swedish university, but above all, I think it is important to speak to as many people as possible to get a flavor of the varieties of any language. It is hard work and you have to learn to polish your language. Read aloud to get the feel of it. Find a voice in your second language. That is not so easy, because the past belongs to another country, another language. Presumably, you have spent your early childhood somewhere else and then acquired a new language on the way. Where is the child in you and the games of childhood in the new language? Test your writing on someone with the second language as a mother tongue. Be critical but at the same time be aware that your voice is also valid in the world of literature.

Adrienne Lecter

Adrienne Lecter has a background in biochemistry and molecular biology, loves ranting at inaccuracies in movies, and spends increasingly more time on the shooting range. She lives in Vienna with the man and two cats in her life, and is working on the next books in the Green Fields series. You can find out more on her website at http://adriennelecter.com

1. Why Do You Write in English?

Back in school, my English teacher convinced me to start reading books in their original English versions (by insinuating to my mother that I was good, but she knew there was so much more unfulfilled potential, and I'm competitive enough for this to make me think, "Now I'll show her!"). Once I realized just how bad the German translations were, there was no going back. I wanted the characters to be as the authors intended, not as the German publishers or translators saw them. And after years and years of predominantly consuming English media, I started writing in English as well. Can you imagine writing a romantic scene in German, the least romantic language there is? No question, wordsmiths like Goethe, or the modern minds behind Rammstein and Die Fantastischen Vier can craft phenomenal literary creations, but English is a much more fluent language to write fiction in than German.

2. How Does Writing in another language influence your work? Or does it? Is there a difference?

Yes, there is a difference. German lends itself to very convoluted, bordering on stilted, sentences. English flows much more freely, so it's perfect for snappy banter and quick action scenes. I also feel like my "writing headspace" has become English since everything I read or watch is in English as well. I don't translate from German when I write; the visuals and sentences in my mind form in English. Every book I read, every interview I listen to, my mind soaks up the sentences like a sponge, readying them for later use when I sit down at the keyboard.

3. What advice would you give to an author who would like to write in a second (or even third or fourth) language?

Completely immerse yourself in the language. You don't have to live in a country where that language is spoken, but you can choose to read, listen, and watch content in your chosen language. YouTube, podcasts, eBooks—the possibilities are endless and at the tips of your fingers as long has you have access to the internet.

And then start to write.

It will be hard at first, and might be incredibly cringeworthy down the line, but you didn't become a storyteller overnight, and you won't become a great writer in a second or third language just like that, either. You need to put in the work, and accept help wherever it is offered. Writing groups are good, but fan-fiction communities offer hundreds of readers who are not afraid to correct you if you ask for their help. It has taken me a few years to turn my academic English into the flowing form required by fiction, but it was time well spent.

OVER TO YOU!

I hope, together with the tips from my fellow "foreign" writers, I have given you inspiration to go ahead and write in another language.

The best way to start something is just to go ahead and do it. It's true that writing in another language needs a little more checking and editing than if you were to write in your own tongue. However, there are also many positive aspects to writing in another language.

As an author who can write in more than one language and is familiar with different cultures, you are well placed to describe the human condition in fresh ways. You can gain a certain sense of detachment from the subject matter and you can take your readers to another place that they may not have experienced in the same way as you, a native, have.

So, go ahead, take the plunge and begin writing in another language!

WRITE YOUR STORY

TURN YOUR LIFE INTO FICTION IN TEN EASY STEPS

Do you want to write your own life story but don't know how to turn real events into fiction?

In *Write Your Story* Helena Halme shows you:

- How to get inspired
- How to write with confidence
- How to create strong characters
- How to use dynamic dialogue

"Short how-to that inspires the writer hidden within!"

***Write Your Story* is now out.**

A FREE BOOK

You can now sign up to my Readers' Group mailing list and get a free copy of ***The Young Heart***, a novella based on a true love story from Finland.

***"Wonderfully intimate and honest."* Pauliina Ståhlberg, Director of The Finnish Institute in London.**

Is she too young to fall in love? A standalone read, *The Young Heart* is a prequel to the acclaimed 1980s fiction series, *The Nordic Heart*. Go to www.helenahalme.com to find out more.

ALSO BY HELENA HALME

Write Your Story: Turn Life Into Fiction in 10 Easy Steps

The Nordic Heart Series:

The Young Heart (Prequel)

The English Heart (Book 1)

The Faithful Heart (Book 2)

The Good Heart (Book 3)

The True Heart (Book 4)

The Nordic Heart Box Set (Books 1-4)

The Christmas Heart (Book 5)

Love on the Island Series:

The Island Affair (Book 1)

Coffee and Vodka: A Nordic Family Drama

The Red King of Helsinki: Lies, Spies and Gymnastics

ACKNOWLEDGMENTS

This is my second nonfiction book. I've previously written academic text, which I used to find very hard, but I did, to my huge amazement, win a prize for my thesis. I'd like to thank John Nurminen for the award and for encouraging me to consider writing as a career. It took over two decades for me to finally do it, but, hey, better late than never!

When, last year, I decided to turn a series of lectures and blog posts into *Write Your Story: Turn Your Life into Fiction in Ten Easy Steps*, I found a new format and outlet for writing. Now I am quite in love with setting down my thoughts and sharing my experiences, so watch this space.

As usual, however, producing a book requires a lot of help and patience from several other people. I want to thank my editor, Dorothy Stannard, who has been patient and diligent. Huge thanks must also go to Heidi Amsinck, Freddie P. Peters, Eivor Martinus, and last but not least Adrienne Lecter. These writers have bared their souls to me as well as supported my writing efforts through the years.

Finally, I couldn't have written a word without my first, faithful reader, David Frise. As well as a brilliant proofreader, he is a loving husband, my best friend, and an excellent cook, keeping both my mind and body nourished.

ABOUT THE AUTHOR

Helena Halme grew up in Tampere, Finland, and moved to the UK via Stockholm and Helsinki in her twenties. She's a former BBC journalist, magazine editor, and bookseller.

Since gaining an MA in Creative Writing at Bath Spa University, Helena has published two nonfiction and nine fiction titles, including five in *The Nordic Heart* series.

Read Helena's blog at www.helenahalme.com, where she shares more of her writing tips. Helena is also a mentor, helping other creatives write, publish and market their books.

45869807R00080

Printed in Poland
by Amazon Fulfillment
Poland Sp. z o.o., Wrocław